AND GOD SAID...

MARTHA TANNER

AuthorHouse™
1663 Liberty Drive
Bloomington, IN 47403
www.authorhouse.com
Phone: 1-800-839-8640

Published by AuthorHouse 11/9/2012

ISBN: 978-1-4567-3691-0 (sc)
978-1-4685-8966-5 (e)

Library of Congress Control Number: 2011907650

And God Said…

By

Martha Tanner, author
Carol Shepherd, illustrator

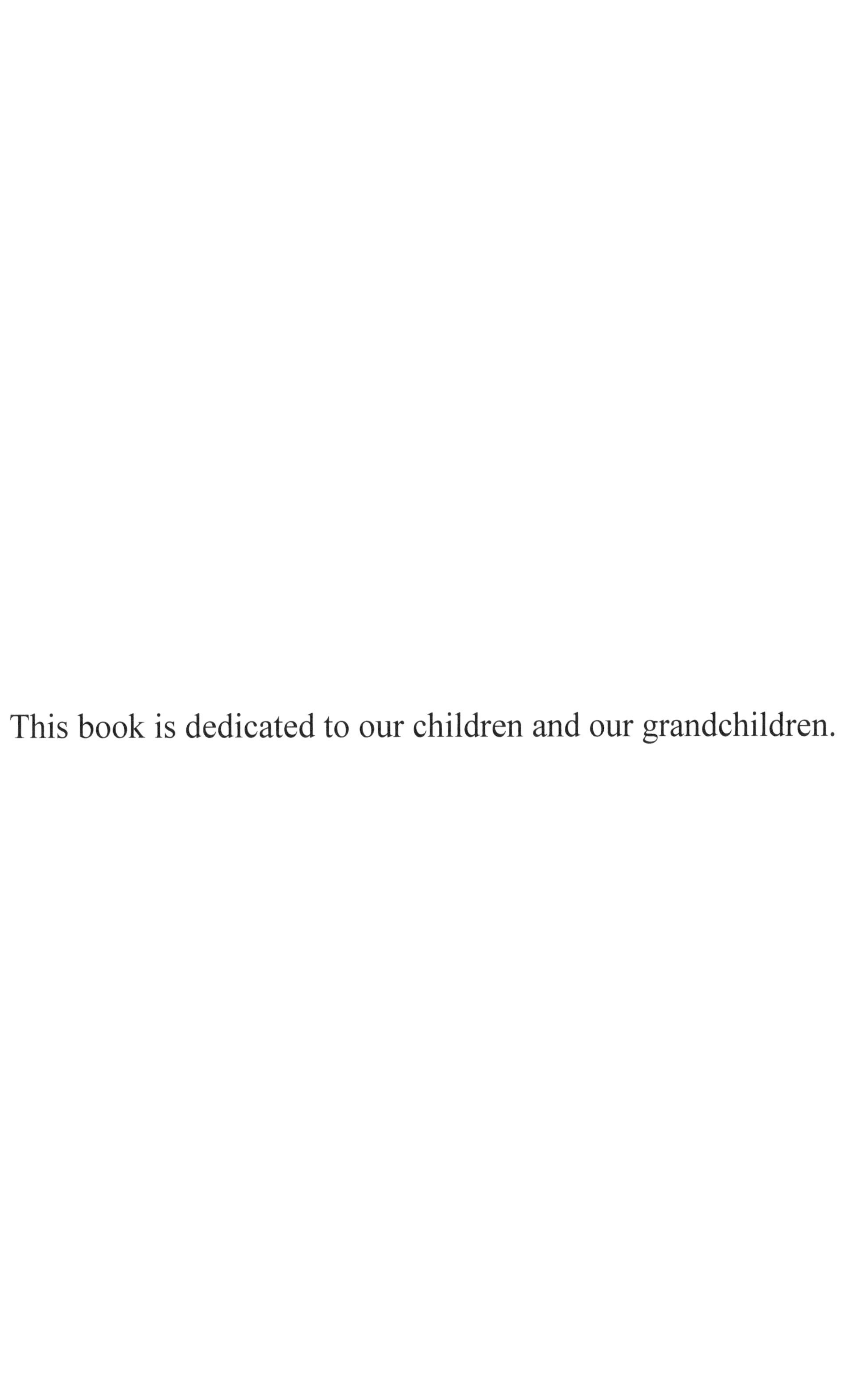

This book is dedicated to our children and our grandchildren.

A long time ago, there weren't any mountains or trees, ladybugs or whales, blades of grass or tiny snails.

NOTHING ....

but

GOD

was

there.

And God said ....

Let there be light and there was light. Light so nice and bright.

God saw that this was good and that was on the first day.

And God said ....

Let there be a sky, and there was a sky. A sky so blue and wide and high.

God saw that this was good and that was on the second day.

And God said ....
Let there be a sun for the day.

A moon and many, many stars for the night.

And God said ....

Let the water go together and make some seas. We'll also need some dry ground. Good things can come from both of these.

God saw that this was good.

And God said ....

Let the land grow corn, beans, carrots, and all the food we eat. Each plant and tree has its own special seed, giving us all the food we need.

God saw that this was good and that was on the third day.

God saw that we needed seasons - Spring, Winter, Summer, and Fall. A changing time for one and all.

God saw that this was good and that was on the fourth day.

And God said ....

Let there be birds that fly and fish that swim. Each and every one made special by Him.

God saw that this was good and that was on the fifth day.

And God said ....

Let there be animals ... All kinds of animals, lions, elephants, pigs, cows, and sheep. Animals that crawl and creatures that creep.

And God said ....

Let us make man. Then out of the ground he made man just right, and with His breath He gave him life. A little later God made man a wife.

And God said ....

Your name will be Adam,
and how busy you'll be.
For I want you to watch
over my animals, plants,
and every tree.

God saw that all He made was good, very good. And that was on the sixth day.

And God said ....
Let there be a time for rest.
A time to do what is best.

And that was on the seventh day.

www.ingramcontent.com/pod-product-compliance
Ingram Content Group UK Ltd.
Pitfield, Milton Keynes, MK11 3LW, UK
UKHW060122300726
14090UKWH00002B/321

* 9 7 8 1 4 5 6 7 3 6 9 1 0 *